# SOCIAL W            :
# A SP
# PERSPECTIVE

*Paul L. Knox*

*Oxford University Press, Ely House, London W. 1*

GLASGOW  NEW YORK  TORONTO  MELBOURNE  WELLINGTON
CAPE TOWN  IBADAN  NAIROBI  DAR ES SALAAM  LUSAKA  ADDIS ABABA
DELHI  BOMBAY  CALCUTTA  MADRAS  KARACHI  LAHORE  DACCA
KUALA LUMPUR  SINGAPORE  HONG KONG  TOKYO

ISBN 0 19 874039 5

© Oxford University Press 1975

Printed in Great Britain
by J. W. Arrowsmith Ltd., Bristol

# Social Well-being:
# A Spatial Perspective

PAUL L. KNOX

Theory and Practice in Geography

OXFORD UNIVERSITY PRESS · 1975

# Preface

One of the fundamental objectives of human geography should be to determine spatial variations in human welfare, yet until recently little of its literature has directly considered questions of this nature. Now, with an increasing call for 'relevance' in geographic inquiry, there is a great need for an assessment of the concepts and techniques available for describing and analysing spatial variations in well-being. The present work introduces the study of local well-being within the social sciences framework afforded by the 'social indicators' movement.

Such a brief introduction cannot cover every aspect of what is a very wide area of study. Attention is focused on the development of descriptive measures of local well-being with particular reference to public policies and decision-making in Britain. Even within these terms of reference, the discussion of some topics must be limited, whilst others are ignored. Nevertheless, it is hoped that this study will go some way towards illuminating the disparate and unjust patterns of prosperity, welfare, and opportunity within contemporary Britain, as well as illustrating the conceptual and methodological difficulties involved in monitoring such variations.

I am grateful to the many friends and associates who have helped me in the writing and editing of this publication. Special acknowledgement is due to Bryan Coates, Senior Lecturer in Geography at the University of Sheffield, who has been a constant source of advice and encouragement since the beginning of my postgraduate career. Thanks are also due in this conext to Professor S. Gregory and Mr. G. M. Lewis of the Department of Geography at Sheffield. In preparing the manuscript, I am indebted to the series editor, Professor J. W. House, for invaluable advice on the content and structure of the work, any shortcomings of which are entirely my own responsibility.

June 1974                                                                P. L. K.

# Contents

# 1 Introduction

In a number of the more prosperous countries of the world, economic development and levels of consumption have reached a point where the marginal utility of consumer goods and services is beginning to decrease. Accordingly, patterns of demand have extended to embrace satisfactions which are often more collective and qualitative in nature, such as those related to environmental quality, social welfare, and recreational facilities. At the same time, there has been a growing concern for those sections of the community whose relative lack of command over resources and lack of opportunity and power leave them the victims, rather than beneficiaries, of economic growth. These attitudes are reflected in the frequency of mass media features and discussions on the environment, homelessness, delinquency, equality of job opportunity, and so on. In turn this publicity has increased the awareness of the national and local electrorate, who are now demanding a greater degree of citizen participation and a more effective approach to social problems.

In response to these changes, central governments in Europe and North America are accepting an increasing responsibility for many aspects of personal welfare, environmental quality, and economic opportunity. Moreover, in relation to the broader aims of government policies, the emphasis is shifting from the promotion of economic growth to the improvement of the 'quality of life'. As a result, the spatial outcome of public policies will increasingly be judged in terms of improvements of the *over-all* well-being of the residents of neighbourhoods, cities, and regions, rather than just in terms of economic activity and efficiency. Indeed, such objectives are already explicit in many policy documents and planning recommendations. In Britain, most territorial policies now subscribe, at least in token form, to the aim of improving local well-being not only in relation to industrial location, land use, and transportation, but also in relation to health, education, and social welfare. The most obvious illustration of the reorientation of policy is in the development of thinking on 'deprived' areas, which for a long time have been defined and tackled in terms of inadequate physical conditions. Improved physical conditions, it was thought, would lead directly to improved social conditions. But, as Cullingworth (1972) points out, identical physical environments (whether good or bad) can be associated with totally different social conditions. Recently, however, the importance of social factors has been recognized in government legislation, which has provided a statutory basis for projects such as the Educational Priority Areas programme and the Urban Aid programme to deal with deprived areas in terms of 'multiple deprivation' and 'special social needs'. Other examples of a concern for social issues are not hard to find. The restructuring of local government in Britain, for example, has from the outset been intended not only to increase administrative cohesion and efficiency but also to facilitate increases in the health, security, and general well-being of people living within the new local authority units. Thus among the virtues of the scheme outlined by the Royal Commission on Local Government in England (the Redcliffe-Maud Report) were the promise of 'greatly improved service to the public, both in providing a better environment and in taking care of the needs of individual people and families' and the 'likelihood that people will recognize the relevance of local government to their own and to their neighbour's well-being' (Royal Commission on Local Government in England, 1969: 143).

These changes in attitudes and priorities by the public and the government have led to the need for a drastic improvement in the standard of social reporting. We already have a reasonably detailed and reliable series of economic statistics, but if we are to pursue a more vigorous approach to social and socio-spatial planning we need more information on the state of the social system in order to enable us to enumerate the most urgent problems and formulate policies accordingly. Furthermore, we need a regular and comprehensive system of social reporting in order to gauge the effectiveness of these policies. In the first instance, this requires a large amount of data on social conditions, data which at present do not exist or are insufficiently ordered. Some progress towards establishing an improved range of social statistics has already been made, however. Government agencies in the United States, Britain, and France have been working on the development of 'social indicators' since the late 1960s, and both academics and administrators have become interested in 'monitoring' the state of society through information systems based on sets of social indicators.

## Geography and well-being

Although most of the attention devoted to social conditions and the general well-being of society has been focused at the national level, the spatial component of well-being is of central importance, not only to geographers and planners, but also to society as a whole. Thus, as Smith (1973a) points out, since we do not expect to discriminate against people on the basis of race, religion, colour, or social class, neither should we discriminate against people on the basis of area of residence. Territorial discrimination may be less individualistic in its manifestations and have less immediate effects than, for example, racial discrimination, but it should be equally important to a society which claims to be egalitarian, as most Western societies do. Moreover, measures of national well-being are aggregates of the diverse conditions experienced by individuals and therefore mask extremes of 'good' and 'bad' which are experienced in different locations as well as by members of different occupational, social, and demographic groups.

Generally speaking, however, geographers have paid little attention to spatial variations in social conditions within advanced industrial countries. It is a particularly unfortunate omission on the part of British geographers when set against the long-established background of interest in spatial aspects of social welfare originating with Charles Booth, fostered by Geddes, Barlow, Beveridge, and Titmuss, and implicit in the post-war regional policies of Government. Concentrations of social, demographic and familial instability in the 'zone of transition' around the core of urban areas have been recognized and investigated by urban geographers since the emergence of the 'Chicago School' of urban social ecology in the 1930s. But in addition to these intra-urban variations in social conditions there are important inter-urban and inter-regional variations. Within Britain, for example, the incidence of overcrowded dwellings in industrial cities such as Sunderland and Gateshead is commonly up to five times greater than that in more prosperous cities such as Norwich and Brighton; infant mortality rates are approximately twice as high in Lancashire and the West Riding of Yorkshire as in south-eastern England; and the proportion of oversized classes in junior schools ranges from less than 5 per cent in rural Wales to over 30 per cent in many urban local education authority areas. Recently, such variations have attracted an increasing amount of attention. Moser and Scott (1961), in an important work on the social and economic characteristics of British towns, were able to demonstrate the nature and extent of inter-urban disparities, whilst Coates and Rawstron (1971) have analysed the extent of regional disparities in a large number of aspects of affluence, opportunity of employment, health, and education. Publications such as these have gone some way to redressing the balance between economic and social themes in human geography. Moreover, there are signs that 'humanistic' concepts such as environmental quality, social well-being, and the quality of life will be as prominent in geographic research in the 1970s as the concepts of economic development and economic health were in the 1960s. One of the chief proponents of a more socially oriented discipline is D. M. Smith, who has argued persuasively for a geography of social well-being (Smith 1973a) and outlined a welfare approach which could provide a useful focus for human geography (Smith 1973b). Such an approach avoids the danger of regarding economic and social topics as separate 'boxes' competing for the geographer's attention. Furthermore, it recognizes economic efficiency as a means of improving social conditions rather than as an end in itself.

The most effective stimulus to the development of a humanistic 'welfare geography' is likely to come from the demands of public policy. Improving the well-being of specific neighbourhoods, cities, or regions requires some means of accurately describing spatial variations in well-being so that policies can be formulated and later assessed efficiently. The present study outlines the development of descriptive measures of local well-being with particular reference to public policies and decision-making in Britain. A review of the 'social indicators movement' serves to introduce a discussion of the scope and utility of territorial social in indicators (Chapter 2). The conceptual framework for territorial social indicators afforded by the notion of 'level of living' is then examined, previous applications are described, and a working definition of level of living applicable to contemporary British conditions is set out (Chapter 3). This is followed by the summary of a preliminary attempt to measure the extent of spatial variations in level of living within England and Wales (Chapter 4). By way of conclusion, Chapter 5 outlines the potential of a regular, policy-related system of measuring spatial variations in well-being and summarizes the problems involved in establishing such a system.

# 2    Social indicators and public policy

'To do better, we must have some way
of distinguishing better from worse'.
(Rivlin, 1971: 146.)

The increasing emphasis that is being placed on the improvement of well-being as a major goal of public policies of many kinds has inevitably raised the question of how we are to recognize such improvements when they occur. Without some means of measuring relative well-being, we have no way of assessing the effectiveness of these policies in achieving such a broad objective. We have already seen that British government policies relating both to local government reform and regional development are ultimately concerned with over-all improvements in the socio-economic environment. But whilst there is likely to be little difficulty in recognizing, for example, a change in the efficiency of regional administration following the reform of local government, or in identifying the effect of regional policies on industrial location decisions, the more widespread implications of policy implementations are likely to be unresolved unless we have access to an adequate barometer of well-being.

Traditionally, the national and regional well-being of Western societies has been assessed by reference to indices of consumption or production of goods and services, supplemented by income levels, and rates of unemployment and industrial growth. Indeed, after the establishment of Keynesian economics in the early 1950s, aggregate measures of economic preformance such a gross national product rapidly became almost sacrosanct. One result of this was that politicians, administrators, planners, and the mass media, familiar with these quantitative measures and seeing economic prosperity as a solvent for all social ills, employed them as the yardsticks of progress in its widest sense. Economists have always been aware of the technical limitations of these yardsticks, but when they are applied to problems other than the evaluation of changes in consumption or production, the limitations become not only technical but also conceptual. National accounting systems were simply not designed to measure changes in our over-all socio-economic environment, and it is clear that there are many elements of people's well-being (health, leisure, and security, for example) which they do not attempt to represent.

Moreover, many of the increases in production and consumption which are entered entirely on the credit side of national accounting systems can lead to significant decreases in well-being; for example, despite generating investment and production, industrialization is also directly responsible for exacerbating problems of health, environmental pollution and recreational opportunity. In many ways, the discrepancy between the national accounting concepts and current notions of well-being reflects changes in our values. In advanced industrial societies, demands have for many years exceeded 'subsistence' or 'minimum' levels of nutrition, shelter, clothing, etc., and as more and more materialistic demands have been satisfied, public attention has tended to shift towards less tangible goals such as a 'safer society' and a 'cleaner environment'. In effect, the marginal utility of consumer goods and services has decreased, and patterns of demand have extended to embrace satisfactions which are less individualistic and often qualitative in nature. At the same time, the publicity given to the so-called 'ecological crisis' and 'urban crisis' presently confronting Western societies has amply demonstrated that well-being goes beyond some aggregate level of consumption of consumer goods and services.

When then is a barometer of well-being to measure? Well-being is taken here to refer to the *satisfaction of the needs and wants of the population.* Unfortunately, this immediately thrusts upon us the question of what is meant by needs and how it should be measured. Need, like poverty, is a relative concept. For each element of well-being (health, housing, etc.) we can attempt to define minimum quantities and qualities that we equate with needs, but these minima will vary according to prevailing value systems and norms. Accepting this, need can be determined in a number of ways (Harvey 1973). Perhaps the most straightforward way is by consultation with experts (physicians, public health inspectors, social workers, etc.) whose judgement and experience would be relied upon to specify the minima that define need in particular fields. Such an approach may be seen by some to be unjustifiably élitist. One alternative would be to analyse the factors which generate particular categories of need; for example, 'health problems can be related to age, life-cycle, amount of migration and so on. . . . Health problems can also be related to local environmental conditions (density of population, local ecology, air and water quality, and so on). If we knew enough about all these relationships we should be able to predict the volume and incidence of health care problems.' (Harvey, 1973: 104.) If we can do this, then we can also predict the need for health care facilities. The drawback of course is that we are rarely in a position to model such relationships adequately. A third approach relies on the premise that consumer behaviour is a direct reflection of need: goods, services, and amenities whose provision does not match market demand are assumed to reflect unfulfilled needs. This, however, tends to underestimate need in sectors where demand is inhibited by low incomes or imperfect knowledge.

In order to avoid some of these problems, it may be preferable to determine need in terms of feelings of 'relative deprivation'. Individuals are relatively deprived (and therefore feel need) if they want some good, service, or amenity which they regard as feasible, which is available to others, but which is not (at present) available to themselves (Runciman, 1966). This notion of relative deprivation is one which conveniently combines both needs and wants; moreover, it is easily extended from the level of the individual to that of a community or reference group, thus facilitating the assessment of need for neighbourhoods, cities, or regions. But, as Harvey (1973) reminds us, felt needs are not always equivalent to real needs. In some situations, ignorance or misinterpretation can lead poorly served groups to have minimal felt needs. In other words, they do not feel deprived because they do not recognize the possibility of being better off. None of these methods of determining need then is without disadvantages. Harvey suggests that the needs associated with different elements of well-being may best be determined in different ways. Thus 'it may be best to determine consumer need through conventional supply and demand analysis, recreational needs through relative deprivation analysis, housing needs through statistical analysis, and medical care needs through resolution of expert opinion' (Harvey, 1973: 105).

Such considerations, however, are somewhat removed from reality. The present level of sophistication in social reporting falls considerably short of measuring levels of satisfaction against specific parameters of need, however defined. So, for the time being at least, those concerned with well-being must be content with comparative rather than absolute measures. Furthermore, until we know more about collective preferences and priorities, such measures must be based on those categories of needs and wants that are seen by academics and administrators to constitute well-being. Whilst these clearly include the consumer goods and services

that would be registered in the national accounts, they also extend to a
diverse series of social and environmental factors such as social stability
and environmental quality, as well as more fundamental socio-economic
factors such as the provision and quality of housing, medical care, and
access to local and regional amenities.

## Social Indicators

It is only recently, however, that there has been a widespread realiz-
ation that the traditional national accounting concepts are able to reflect
only some of the elements of prosperity, welfare, and opportunity relevant to our general well-being. The subsequent desire for more effective
indicators of well-being has been reflected in the 'social indicators movement', which began in the United States in the mid-1960s and has since
spread across both the Atlantic and the Pacific. Social indicators can be
loosely defined as aggregate or composite measures of well-being, or of
some element of it, and are generally designed to facilitate concise and
comprehensive judgements about levels of social welfare. In most cases
they are aimed at improving information systems for decision-making: to
assess what is happening, to pave the way for policy decisions, and to
monitor the effect of policies. There is now a strong interest in developing
social indicators at the national level within a number of countries. In
Japan, for example, the Sanwa Bank has attempted to compare national
well-being with that of other advanced industrial nations by means of a
'happiness index'. In Britain, France, and the United States, official
governmental agencies are involved in attempts to develop social indicators capable of forming the basis of a system of social accounting
comparable in depth and efficiency to existing national economic accounting systems. Ultimately the hope is to generate a set of indicators which
could be related to national policies in much the same way as economic
indicators such as the cost-of-living index have been developed in order
to help guide economic policy.

Most of the research in this field has been conducted in the United
States and is largely the result of the North American Space Administration's desire for quantitative measures of the 'social spin-off' of its
activities. Some preliminary findings were published in 1966, and within
three years social indicators had established a firm footing in federal
administrative thinking. First, in January 1969, the United States Depart-

ment of Health, Education and Welfare published the seminal document *Towards a Social Report*, which declared official interest in the development of national social indicators. Six months later, the newly elected President Nixon created the National Goals Research Staff, to be responsible for developing social indicators capable of monitoring and predicting the quality of American life.

Since 1969 a considerable amount of literature has appeared on the subject of social indicators. In Britain, most of the impetus has come from statisticians in government, whose official contribution to the field has been the regular publication of *Social Trends*, a package of statistical series relating to social conditions, which endeavours to present a 'rounded picture of British Society' (Moser, 1970). In addition the Social Science Research Council has sponsored an investigation of the use of social indicators with particular emphasis on policy-making in health, crime, and education (Shonfield and Shaw, 1972). The results of this work afford a cautious optimism that effective social indicators may soon exist beyond the wishful thinking of social scientists and social administrators; but, with such a new and rapidly expanding field of interest, it is not surprising to find that there are numerous problems of definition, measurement, and integration to overcome. It is therefore worth clarifying some of the more desirable characteristics of social indicators in order to allow a more meaningful usage of the term. Ideally, social indicators:

1. should be *comprehensive* or aggregate measures of social conditions or of some major aspect of them such as racial equality or juvenile crime.

2. should be available as a *time series*

3. should be easily disaggregated by *geographical area*

4. should, where possible, refer to the *outputs* of the system such as educational achievement, rather than inputs such as expenditure on education, and

5. should relate to public policy *goals* (such as 'equal opportunity' and 'public order and safety').

At present, few social indicators are able to fulfil all these criteria, since they are still very much in their infancy. Moreover, the goals of public policy are often inexplicit and sometimes controversial, whilst the necessary data remain unsatisfactory or incomplete.

It has been suggested that the term social indicator should be restricted to those measures which can be related to a sociological model of some kind (Land, 1970). One of the major reasons for this is that if we are ever to have a sensitive, policy-oriented system of social indicators with which to monitor social conditions, we must first have a 'systems' model of society to serve as a guide as to (1) what aspects of society should be measured, and (2) how the information might best be integrated into a system of measurement. At face value, this presents few difficulties: it is easy enough to view society as a complex, flexible, goal-seeking system. But any attempt to detail an operational model along these lines necessitates the recognition of the active components of the system, which in turn can only be achieved with a sound conceptual and theoretical background. It is the lack of such a background that has hampered the development of social indicators both in Britain and elsewhere. Current social theory offers no solution, whilst the conceptual basis of social indicators has remained vague. Moser suggests that they have come to be generally regarded as being relevant to, and conterminous with, 'all that relates to the quality of life' (Moser, 1971), Similarly, Kamrany and Christakis argue that, for a social indicator (or *system* of social indicators) to be complete, it must embody 'all variables and elements that impinge on the quality of a good life' (Kamrany and Christakis, 1970): what is meant by the quality of life, however, has nowhere been clearly defined. Certainly the situation is not helped by the apparent proliferation of synonyms: level of living, standard of living, social well-being, social welfare, and level of satisfaction all allude to the same general notion of well-being as the quality of life, but all have different connotations or implications. Smith throws some light on the matter when he suggests that 'it may be preferable to regard it [social well-being] as being at the more concrete or specific end of a continuum of abstraction that descends from human happiness through the concept of the quality of life to social well-being' (Smith, 1973a: 66); but he does not go on to elucidate the differentiating factors between the various concepts. Alternatively, Knox (1974a, 1974b) has suggested that level of living provides the best conceptual framework for the development of social indicators. For the present, however, we are necessarily concerned with social indicators which are built around different members of this family of concepts according to the purpose and disposition of their author.

## Territorial social indicators

The bulk of published literature on social indicators to date has been addressed to the question of creating a set of social indicators at the national level. The idea of disaggregating national social indicators by geographical area has been implicit in most of this work, but relatively few attempts have been made either to explore the idea in detail or to construct territorial social indicators. However, since the central concern of this book lies in the *spatial* expression of well-being, particular attention is given here to those attempts to operate social indicators within a spatial framework. As with national social indicators, most of the progress in this field arises from research undertaken in the United States; nevertheless, most of the findings are relevant to the British context and worthy of examination in some detail. The technical and conceptual problems associated with territorial social indicators are discussed in a number of papers (Kamrany and Christakis, 1970; Perle, 1970; Terleckyj, 1970), but the reader is referred to Smith (1973a) for the most comprehensive treatment of the subject. Smith's work on the geography of social well-being in the United States also represents the most important contribution to the actual *construction* of territorial social indicators and, moreover, marks an important step in the development of a socially responsible human geography.

Territorial social indicators are not merely a product of the geographer's perspective on the general social-indicators movement; they are a necessary and logical extension of any realistic system of social reporting. People live locally and experience the prosperity, stresses, expectations, and satisfactions of their own locality. National social indicators are aggregates of these conditions and as such may mask important problems at the local level. Furthermore, across-the-board policies aimed at improving some aspect of over-all national well-being often aggravate rather than improve the situation at the local level. The classic example of this can be found in the application of expansionary national fiscal and monetary policies designed to reduce unemployment: whilst unemployment rates are reduced in areas of underemployment, the economy of more prosperous areas becomes acutely overheated. In short, 'blanket' national social and economic policies are inadequate: to be effective, policies must be implemented and monitored at the local level.

The responsibility of local authorities for various aspects of social welfare in their areas is a further reason for constructing territorial social indicators. In Britain, counties, county boroughs and some smaller administrative units are able to contribute significantly to the standards of health, housing, education, law and order, and environmental quality achieved by the communities within their jurisdiction. It is particularly important, therefore, to develop social indicators geared to the specific needs and goals of these decision-making units.

### Some practical considerations

In the construction of territorial social indicators the first consideration is to decide upon the spatial framework to be used. There should be a close correspondence between the sub-areas used for these indicators and the sub-areas relevant to public policy implementation. Fortunately, this fits in well with the necessarily pragmatic approach from the point of view of data availability, since in most countries administrative units provide the basis for the bulk of all socio-economic data.

Several difficulties arise from the use of such units, however. Their properties as data-collecting units give rise to fundamental problems of presentation and analysis which are familiar to most geographers (Duncan, Cuzzort, and Duncan, 1961; King, 1969). In particular, it is important always to bear in mind that territorial social indicators based on administrative units are reflective only of *aggregate* conditions at a particular level of resolution. Another important practical consideration is the approach to measurement adopted in constructing territorial social indicators. Generally, the approach will depend upon the subject-matter, the quality of available data, and the purpose of the exercise. Kamrany and Christakis (1970) suggested that regional social and environmental conditions can be translated into three different kinds of indicators, determined largely by subject-matter: (1) absolute indicators; (2) relative indicators; and (3) autonomous indicators.

Absolute indicators are used where there is substantial 'scientific' agreement over maximum or minimum levels necessary to certain aspects of well-being. Examples include minimum requirements for clean air and minimum levels of protein or calorie intake. This approach to measurement is intuitively appealing, since a good deal of objectivity is implied, and difficulties of interpretation are minimized.

Relative indicators are used when no optimum value is available and simply give a measure of the relative condition of different regions or areas. Examples can be drawn from most aspects of housing, health, leisure, social stability, and material affluence. In fact, most aspects of well-being can only be measured by way of relative indicators because the available data offer no alternative. The problem thus becomes one of selecting the most appropriate variables with which to construct relative indicators. The use of social indicators therefore inevitably involves value judgements, a fact often overshadowed by the 'objectivity' implied by the technicalities of combining and weighting the variables to form indicators.

Autonomous indicators are specific to conditions in areas with social, economic, or cultural values differing from those prevalent in the over-all territory. In Britain such indicators are relevant only at the micro-scale: to Asian communities in Bradford or Glasgow, for instance.

A more useful classification of social indicators has been put forward by Carlisle (1972), who identifies four types:

1. *Informative indicators*, which are essentially descriptive of social conditions at a particular point in time and, ideally, available as a time series. They are intended to cover the whole social system and therefore require some prior decision as to those aspects of well-being which need to be measured.

2. *Predictive indicators*, which are informative indicators linked to a model or theory of social change, so that changes in the indicators infer changes in social or socio-spatial processes. The development of such indicators is clearly a long-term prospect, dependent in the first instance on the development of successful informative indicators.

3. *Problem-oriented indicators*, which are quantitative expressions of particular problems (such as 'educational deprivation' and 'housing stress') designed to provide the basis for policy decisions by identifying concentrations of social problems.

4. *Programme-evaluation indicators*, which are intended to monitor the progress and effectiveness of policies by quantifying social conditions in relation to some predetermined target.

These categories are not mutually exclusive, but they do offer a convenient classification according to the use of an indicator within a general information system. At present, few attempts have been made to construct predictive or programme-evaluation indicators, attention having been focused more on problem-oriented and informative indicators. On the whole, local and central government agencies have been concerned with developing the former, whilst academics have been more closely involved in attempts to assess well-being by way of informative indicators based on concepts such as the quality of life, social well-being, and level of living.

## Problem-oriented indicators

An excellent example of a problem-oriented social indicator designed to operate in a spatial context is that of the index developed by the Inner London Education Authority (I.L.E.A.) in order to identify schools and neighbourhoods for designation in Educational Priority Areas. This work arises directly from the recommendations of the Plowden Report (Central Advisory Council for Education (England), 1967) relating to the need for public intervention in favour of areas 'where educational handicaps are reinforced by social handicaps'. The report urged that various 'objective criteria' should be used to ascertain those schools and neighbourhoods needing special help and to determine how much assistance should be given. The criteria suggested by the report were: poor attendance and truancy; the incidence of retarded, disturbed, or handicapped pupils; the inability of pupils to speak English; the incidence of incomplete (e.g. fatherless) families; the incidence of shared and overcrowded households; the extent of supplements in cash or kind from the State; family size; occupation; and the existence of a high turn-over of pupils or teachers. Central government funds were quickly made available for school building in Educational Priority Areas, and the Department of Education and Science (D.E.S.) invited local authorities to submit their proposals, based on 'such statistical evidence as may be readily available' (Little and Mabey, 1972). The sort of evidence that the D.E.S. was looking for corresponded closely to the criteria set out in the Plowden Report, and also included measures of the physical quality of housing and the environment; but the question of how the evidence should be presented and interpreted was left to individual local authorities.

One of the first authorities to tackle this problem in a comprehensive way was the I.L.E.A., an authority containing within its boundaries some of the worst conditions of multiple deprivation in Britain. Their answer was an index derived from a series of ten carefully selected measures of educational, social, and environmental deprivation and stress. Details of the index are given by Little and Mabey (1972). Basically, the index was a straightforward aggregation of standardized scores on the following variables:

1. % occupied males in semi-skilled and unskilled jobs
2. % pupils receiving free school meals
3. % households overcrowded (living at a density of over 1·5 persons per room)
4. % households without an inside lavatory
5. average rate of absence in junior schools
6. % pupils of low ability (bottom quartile) at the 'eleven plus' transfer stage
7. % immigrant children
8. % teachers with less than 3 years' experience at their current school
9. % pupils not completing a year at any school
10. % children living in households of 6 or more people.

The index was computed for each of 600 schools in the I.L.E.A. area, and has been used within the I.L.E.A. to guide policy decisions as well as in negotiations with the D.E.S. for the allocation of additional resources for school building and teachers' salaries. The actual index values reveal a vicious picture of inequality and restricted opportunities. The situation is summarized by Little and Mabey:

In the school figuring first [worst] on the Index nearly half of the employed men in the immediate area were in semi-skilled or unskilled jobs, half of the children in the area were in large families, one-eighth of the households in the area were technically overcrowded and over one-third of them were without inside lavatories. In school nearly one-third of the children received free school dinners; an average of one-seventh of the children were absent in a selected week, two-thirds of the children were immigrants, three-quarters of the children were placed in the lowest quarter on an ability test, over half of them had had an incomplete year in the school and four out of five teachers in the school had been there for less than three years.

Looking at the 150th school and comparing it with the 'national average', there are only small differences in social class, family size and housing stress. However, more than twice the national average receive free dinners; instead of one immigrant pupil for every forty children it is one for every five. The incidence of teacher turnover is fifty per cent above the national average and pupil turnover is more than twice the national average. Finally, instead of a class of forty having ten pupils of low ability and performance, this school will have sixteen.' (Little and Mabey 1972: 85.)

It is within the field of housing, however, that local authorities have found most use for problem-oriented territorial indicators. Many of the large urban authorities in Britain and the United States employ indicators of 'housing stress', 'residential quality', 'urban decay', and so on as bases for delimiting the boundaries of redevelopment areas, improvement areas action areas, and, in the United States, housing code enforcement programmes. These indicators range in complexity and sophistication from composite dot-maps of indices of social *malaise* (e.g. homelessness, juvenil delinquency, infant mortality) to weighted indices derived from multivariate statistical analyses of specially collected data. Intermediate between these extremes is the index of housing stress developed by the Greater London Council, which is derived from seven census variables:

1. % households living at a density of more than 1·5 persons per room
2. % households with more than 3 people living at a density of more than 1·5 persons per room
3. % households without access to a fixed bath
4. % households in multi-occupation
5. % households without access to hot and cold water supplies
6. % households in multi-occupation housing having no access to their own stove or sink
7. % households of 3 or more persons which are in multi-occupation.

The index was used in the Greater London Development Plan (Greater London Council, 1969) to define Stress Areas. These comprised some 68 wards located mainly in inner London: areas such a Brixton, Camberwell, Clapham, Harlesden, Holloway, Notting Hill, Shoreditch, Wapping, and Willesden (see Fig. 2.1) where inequalities and contrasts resulting from maladjustment, maldistribution, net shortages, sharing, crowding, and lack of basic amenities are compounded by accelerating urban decay, the scarcity of land and resources for renewal, and the special needs of migrants and immigrants. The worst-affected boroughs are Islington, Hackney, Lambeth, Brent, Hammersmith, and Southwark—boroughs which also fare very poorly in terms of indicators of social stress such as the incidence of evictions, children in care, and general homelessness (Lomas, 1973).

In broader context, the Home Office has been developing problem-oriented indicators in order to resolve the question of allocating the scarce funds of the Urban Programme to local authorities and voluntary organizations wanting to finance projects in deprived urban areas. Under

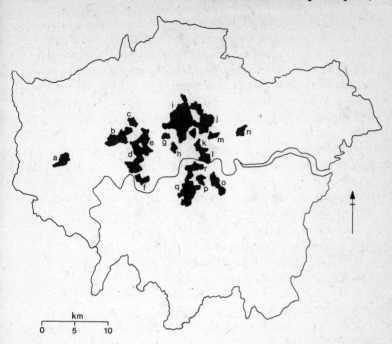

FIG. 2.1   Areas of housing stress in Greater London, 1966. Shaded areas indicate
the 10 per cent of wards with the highest stress index. An indication of
their location is given by the letters:
(a) Southall; (b) Harlesden/Willesden; (c) Dollis Hill; (d) Shepherd's
Bush/Notting Hill; (e) Kilburn; (f) Fulham; (g) Kentish Town; (h) Somers
Town; (i) Finsbury/Highbury/Holloway/South Hornsey/South Tottenham,
(j) Stoke Newington; (k) Shoreditch; (l) Wapping; (m) South Hackney;
(n) West Ham; (o) Deptford; (p) Camberwell; (q) Brixton/Clapham/Tulse
Hill; (r) Newington.
*Source*: After Greater London Council (1969).

the programme, approved projects receive a grant covering 75 per cent
of the costs, and, in view of the conditions in much of urbanized
Britain, it is not surprising to find that the available funds are over-
subscribed by up to ten times. Basically, the programme aims to help
areas suffering from multiple deprivation by improving the local social
services. The Urban Programme is thus a social policy programme using
territorial social indicators to identify 'deprived areas'. According to one
of the team responsible for developing these indicators, 'people living in
deprivation [are] those . . . least able to compete in three major com-
petitive markets—housing, employment and education. . . . Where there
are areal concentrations of inability to compete, there are deprived areas'.
(Edwards, 1973: 21.) This conception of deprivation is operationalized
by the following census variables:

1. % semi-skilled manual workers
2. % unskilled manual workers
3. % economically active males seeking employment
4. % households overcrowded
5. % households sharing their dwelling
6. % households living in privately rented furnished accommodation
7. % persons aged 15—25 living in private households who were not
full-time students

The three employment variables are surrogates for measures of low
pay, job insecurity, and persistent unemployment, whilst the three
housing variables represent an attempt to emphasize the personal and
social aspects of housing deprivation. Variable (6) in particular is seen
by the Home Office team as reflective of those who have 'lost out' and
filtered down the housing market. Data for each of the variables will be
collected for every enumeration district in England and Wales (there are
roughly 100 000 of them) and used to produce four indicators: one for
each of the three major components of deprivation, and a composite
index derived for all seven variables. With these indicators, it is hoped,
it will be possible to identify those areas worthy of Urban Programme
funds.

The three examples of problem-oriented indicators presented here
are not set out as models of their kind, but rather as illustrations of recent attempts to identify spatial concentrations of particular social problems. One important handicap they all share is that the problems they

seek to identify on the ground—educational deprivation, housing stress, and so on—are really rather nebulous and ill-defined. Because of this, the problems themselves are often seen in terms of easily abstracted statistics rather than in terms of social processes and theories. Thus housing stress *becomes* overcrowding, lack of household amenities, and all the usual census variables. These yardsticks are clearly useful at present because they satisfy the immediate demand for social indicators, but there is a danger that they will become entrenched as successive studies justify the composition of their indicators on the basis of precedent. What is required, of course, is fundamental research into the nature and causes of the problems, so that we can progress towards more sensitive indicators of their existence.

In the final analysis, however, problem-oriented indicators must be seen as stop-gap measures. What is needed to assess the effectivemess of public policies is a comprehensive system of indicators which covers all aspects of well-being. In order to develop such a system we must turn our attention to what Carlisle (1972) called 'informative' indicators.

## Informative indicators

Most of the indicators in this category are the result of attempts by academics to obtain some kind of quantified measure of over-all well-being, often couched in terms of the 'quality of life'. Unfortunately, this is also a rather vague concept, usually defined only by the variables used to represent it. An exception in this context is Wilson's study of inter-state variations in the quality of life in the U.S.A. (Wilson, 1969). Wilson was able to get around the problem of interpreting the concept by basing his indicators on the 'domestic goal areas' set out in the Report of the President's Commission on National Goals (1960). Indicators relating to nine goal areas (individual status, individual equality, state and local government, education, economic growth, technological change, agriculture, living conditions, and health and welfare) were derived from a series of variables selected so as to relate to the specific aims of the goal areas. The nature of these indicators can best be understood by simply listing a few of the actual variables. The indicator for the goal area of 'improved living conditions' is derived from eight variables, including per cent of families with income under $3000; per cent of sound housing with plumbing facilities; and per capita general expenditure of state and local government on housing and urban renewal.

More recently Flax (1972) has investigated the quality of life in eighteen large metrololitan areas of the U.S.A. using indicators based on fourteen 'quality categories' held to be relevant to American life. These indicators are only broadly similar in scope to Wilson's, although some of the differences can be attributed to the change in scale from the state to the metropolitan level. Air pollution, for example, is an important factor at the metropolitan level, but becomes less meaningful at the state level. The list of Flax's quality categories includes Unemployment, Income, Housing, Health, Public Order, Racial Equality, Citizen Participation, Educational Attainment, Air Quality, and Social Disintegration, but an examination of the fourteen indicators used by Flax reveals that there is no consideration, implicit or explicit, of important factors such as residential quality, recreational opportunity, and social welfare. To a large extent, this must be due to the lack of a cohesive conceptual framework on which to build the indicators.

In an attempt to establish a degree of consensus as to which conditions an over-all measure of well-being should reflect, Smith (1973a) has analysed the content of ten major works from the social-indicators movement and ten textbooks from the field of social problems. From these, it proved possible to arrive at a broad consensus about well-being:

In a well society people will have incomes adequate for their basic needs of food, clothing, shelter, and a 'reasonable' standard of living; people will not live in poverty. The status and dignity of the individual will be respected, and he will be socially and economically mobile. Good quality education and health services will be available to all, and their use will be reflected in a high level of physical and mental health and in an informed populace able to perform their societal roles in a satisfactory manner. People will live in decent houses, in decent neighbourhoods, and will enjoy a good quality of physical environment. They will have access to recreational facilities, including culture and the arts, and adequate leisure time in which to enjoy these things. Society will show a low degree of disorganization, with few personal social pathologies, little deviant behaviour, low crime incidence, and high public order and safety. The family will be a stable institution, with few broken homes. Individuals will be able to participate in social, economic, and political life and will not be alienated on the basis of race, religion, ethnic origin or any other cause. (Smith, 1973a: 69.)

Using these ideas as a foundation, Smith lists seven general criteria of

'social well-being'—Income, Wealth, and Employment; the Living Environment (housing, physical environment, the neighbourhood); Health;
Education; Social Order (crime, public order, family breakdown, personal
pathologies); Social Belonging (democratic participation, criminal justice,
segregation); and Recreation and Leisure—which serve as a basis for
operational definitions (i.e. sets of variables) that are subsequently used
to determine how social well-being varies spatially at three levels of
resolution—inter-state, inter-city, and intra-city—within the United States.

In Britain, Gordon and Whittaker (1972) developed indicators of
'prosperity' for local areas in the South-West region. Doubting whether
there is any real agreement as to the relative importance of various aspects
of prosperity, Gordon and Whittaker followed a 'compromise' approach
to its measurement. First, on the assumption that average income per head
provides the most useful single indicant of prosperity, attention was
concentrated on its spatial distribution. Secondly, recognizing that there
are other important dimensions of prosperity that ought not to be ignored,
they attempted to identify these dimensions through a multivariate
analysis (factor analysis) of variables representing as many aspects of
economic and social well-being as possible within the range of available
data. The aspects thus covered may briefly be listed:

1. Income
2. Unemployment
3. Seasonality of unemployment
4. Female activity rate
5. Professional and intermediate workers
6. Skilled workers
7. Partly skilled and unskilled
workers
8. Migration of young males
9. Average domestic rateable
value
10. Houses with very low rateable value
11. Households with exclusive
use of all census amenities
12. Cars per household
13. Telephone ownership
14. Post-war housing
15. Owner-occupation
16. Employment growth
17. Growth industries
18. Industrial building
19. Terminal age of education
20. Movement of school leavers
21. Doctors per head
22. Accessibility to services
23. Death rate.

Six major dimensions (factors) emerged from the analysis, but, despite the use of only normative input variables, i.e. variables for which a change in a particular direction along a quantified scale could clearly be recognized as either 'good' or 'bad', the third factor turned out to be ambiguous and was discounted from further consideration. The major dimensions of economic and social well-being were therefore represented by five factors, descriptively identified as 'money', 'property', 'growth', 'opportunity', and 'employment structure' factors respectively. Using the scores for these normative factors to construct a summary map, Gordon and Whittaker were able to identify areas of consistently above- or below-average prosperity. In relation to the pattern that emerged, they note that there is 'little correspondence with the present boundaries of assisted areas, which principally reflect an unemployment criterion' (Gordon and Whittaker, 1972: 308).

Although this sort of observation is clearly aimed at policy-makers in central and local government, Gordon and Whittaker do not see their indicators as sufficiently refined to be directly suitable for use in monitoring the effect of public policies. Nevertheless, their work, together with the background provided by the work of Wilson, Flax, and particularly Smith in the U.S.A., affords a starting-point from which it is possible to develop preliminary measures of territorial well-being for British policy-makers. The immediate concern, however, should be to establish some conceptual basis around which these measures can be built, since it is clear that most attempts to measure well-being have been hampered by the lack of a cohesive and well-defined conceptual framework. The author has suggested that the concept of level of living can provide such a framework (Knox, 1974b). In subsequent chapters the concept is discussed in detail, and is used to illustrate the extent of spatial variations in well-being within England and Wales.

# 3    Level of living: an integrated approach to well-being

'Level of living is a crucial concept for the assessment of the results of development and also for development planning. This is because the purpose of development is the improvement of the conditions in which people live, and the level of living is supposed to be a quantitative expression of these conditions'. (Drewnowski, 1970: 1.)

In contrast to the recent and rather vague notion of the quality of life, the concepts of standard and level of living are relatively well defined and provide an ideal foundation for the development of informative territorial social indicators. Throughout a long doctrinal history in sociology and economics, the concepts have been regarded as convenient frameworks for the analysis of a large number of interrelated elements of social and economic well-being (Pipping, 1953). In view of the widespread interest in social indicators and growing concern for the problems and injustices of territorial disparities in social welfare, it is surprising that geographers and planners have been largely unaware of the potential utility of the concepts as vehicles for research.

Basically, *level of living* may be regarded as the factual circumstances of well-being, the actual degree of satisfaction of the needs and wants of a person or group of persons; whilst the *standard of living* relates to the circumstances aspired to by those persons. More explicit definitions must ultimately depend on the context of their use. Most sociological investigations have derived from the work of the former Bureau of Agricultural Economics of the United States Department of Agriculture, which for many years produced the official Farm Operator Level of Living Index. The index was first published in 1943, and was computed for each county of the United States as a weighted combination of a series of variables, each selected so as to indicate the possession or consumption of as wide a range as possible of goods and services which were 'generally sought by all groups and classes of people'. Until 1950, the variables used in constructing the index were (1) the percentage of farms with electricity, (2) the percentage of farms with a telephone, (3) the percentage of farms with a car, and (4) the average value of farm produce sold or traded in the preceding year. After 1950 the average value of land and buildings per farm replaced the percentage of farms with electricity as one of the four constituents. According to Hagood and Bowles, who were closely concerned with the development of the index, 'the concept of level of living which the indexes are intended to reflect is the average level of current consumption of goods and services (Hagood and Bowles, 1957: 15). Although the indices were not claimed to be comprehensive, this notion of level of living is clearly rather narrow. Nevertheless, the indices were seen by rural sociologists in the 1940s as a useful technique in analyses of social structure. The indices proved particularly effective in illustrating urban—rural contrasts within American society, and there developed a large volume of literature dealing not only with levels of living at the county scale, but also with the investigation and measurementof levels of living among families and neighbourhoods. Much of this work took a broader interpretation of level of living, recognizing, for the first time, important components of the concept, such as leisure, security, and social stability, none of which can be classed as consumers' goods or services.

In 1956 the Rural Sociological Society, reviewing the existing literature on standards and levels of living, concluded that 'standards and levels of living may be empirically represented by an inventory of the physical acoutrements constituting the material and cultural possessions of the people in question; by the values and norms of behaviour which they share; by the forms of social organization which they practise; by the geographic factors which make up the environment in which the people live; and by the effectiveness with which the people in question satisfy the basic needs of food, health, shelter, education, protection for the individual, conditions of work, clothing, etc.', emphasizing that the difference between level and standard of living is that the former 'refers to the actual conditions of life among the people in question', whilst the latter 'refers to the aspiration levels of the people themselves' (Rural Sociological Society, 1956: 183). Having established level of living as a concept reflective of over-all social and economic well-being, however, sociologists have made little use of the concept since the mid-1950s, perhaps because it is descriptive rather than analytic in nature.

In contrast, studies of international social and economic development have increasingly made use of the concept since that time. Research in this field has been pioneered by the United Nations Organization, one of whose aims is to increase the level of living of member nations. In order to ascertain exactly what this objective implied in terms of obligations and responsibilities for the parent organization, the General Assembly directed the Economic and Social Council to appoint a committee to investigate the definition and measurement of levels of living. The committee first reported in 1954, and since then considerable progress has been made towards a policy-related system of measurement. Eventually, it was decided to define level of living in terms of a series of *components*, each intended to represent a distinct class of human needs, the satisfaction of which is measured indirectly by a series of *indicators*. Table 3.1 lists these components and indicators, and illustrates the general design of the United Nations Index of Level of Living. Because of the wide range of cultures and value systems throughout the world, the components represent the common denominators of level of living at the broadest level of resolution. Similarly, the indicators are elementary in character because of the impoverished conditions prevalent throughout most of the world. The indicators were not initially designed as additive measures, but much of the appeal of the concept of level of living lies in its unitary nature, and it is partly for this reason that an over-all index is now preferred by the United Nations as the best means of representation. It is also useful to have a unitary measure for practical reasons. Drewnowski and Scott, who have been closely associated with the development of the United Nations index, argue that 'a unitary index of the level of living can also play an important role in the planning process. When alternative development strategies are considered before decision is taken, a clear overall view of the social consequences of alternative courses of action is best obtained through a properly devised unitary level of living index.' (Drewnowski and Scott, 1968: 266.) Nevertheless, a useful feature of the United Nations index is that, although it provides a unitary measure, it can be disaggregated to give over-all scores for each of the seven components. Fig. 3.1 illustrates this, using as examples three countries whose levels of living are quite different. In advanced industrial countries such as Belgium, high levels of living are the result of a high degree of satisfaction of all needs, with the marked exception of security. In the slightly less-developed countries of the world (e.g. Greece) levels of living are somewhat lower, with relatively high levels of satisfaction of Physical Needs (nutrition, health, shelter) tending to be offset by a moderate satisfaction of Cultural Needs (education, leisure, security) and an even lower degree of satisfaction of

TABLE 3.1

*General Design of the United Nations Level of Living Index*

| Type of Need | Component | Indicator |
|---|---|---|
| A. PHYSICAL | (1) Nutrition | a. Calorie intake per head |
| | | b. Protein intake per head |
| | | c. Proportion of calorie intake derived from cereals, roots, tubers, and sugars |
| | (2) Shelter | a. Quality of habitation |
| | | b. Density of occupancy |
| | | c. Independence of occupancy |
| | (3) Health | a. Access to medical care |
| | | b. Mortality attributable to parasitic and infectious diseases |
| | | c. Proportional mortality ratio |
| B. CULTURAL | (4) Education | a. School enrolment ratio |
| | | b. School output ratio |
| | | c. Pupil–teacher ratio |
| | (5) Leisure and Recreation | a. Average leisure time |
| | | b. Daily newspaper circulation |
| | | c. Incidence of radio and television sets |
| | (6) Security | a. Incidence of violent deaths |
| | | b. Proportion of population covered by unemployment and sickness benefits |
| | | c. Proportion of population covered by retirement schemes |
| C. HIGHER | (7) Surplus Income | a. Income surplus to the satisfaction of basic physical and cultural needs |

*Source:* After Drewnowski and Scott (1968).

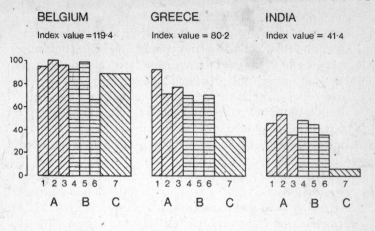

FIG. 3.1   Levels of living in three selected countries, around 1960. A = Physical
           Needs:
           (1) Nutrition, (2) Shelter, (3) Health;
           B = Cultural Needs:
           (4) Education, (5) Leisure, (6) Security;
           C = Higher Needs:
           (7) Surplus Income.
           *Source*: After Drewnowski and Scott (1968).

Higher Needs. Finally, 'third world' countries such as India are charac-
terized by extremely low levels of living, with particularly low scores on
health and security, and an almost negligible degree of satisfaction of
Higher Needs.

## Level of living as a measure of regional well-being

An index such as the one outlined above would clearly be too blunt
an instrument with which to measure variations in well-being within
advanced industrial nations such as Britain. Nevertheless, it serves as an
encouraging precedent: if it is possible to devise an index applicable to
peoples with widely divergent cultures, ideologies, and value systems, it
must surely be possible to develop a more specialized version capable of
gauging variations within a smaller and more consistent universe. Despite
the explicitly spatial nature of international comparisons of level of
living, however, the concept has been employed in few urban or regional
studies. Two such studies are briefly outlined here, whilst a third, by the

author, forms the basis of Chapter 4.

The first of these studies is Lewis's approach to the regional geography of the north-eastern United States. Lewis used the concept of level of living as a means of analysing the population geography of the region. Without defining the concept (beyond an implication that it represents the complex of characteristics which together determine the socio-economic qualities of a population), Lewis operationalized it with a set of twelve variables selected so as to reflect the characteristics of in-migration, education, employment, housing, communication, political awareness, health, and social stability.

Full details of the variables and the subsequent analysis are given in Lewis (1968). Data for each of the variables (by counties) were ranked from 'best' to 'worst' and combined into a relatively simple index, with each variable given equal weighting. Although this method may appear rather arbitrary, careful consideration was given to the selection of the variables, and the resultant index enables a detailed and informative regionalization of the study area to be made. The real value of the index lies in the spatial patterning of the less predictable intermediate scores and in the local anomalies in level of living thrown up by the series of maps which Lewis presents. Lewis concludes that this sort of approach to regional grography has several distinctive merits. In particular, it avoids the dangers of determinism associated with other methods of regionalization in that it 'reverses the conventional order in which the regional geographer treats the several categories of phenomena which combine to give character to place' (Lewis, 1968: 34).

In Britain, the Urban Planning Directorate has used a level-of-living framework in order to assess regional variations in well-being from the point of view of the provision of urban service functions (Ministry of Housing and Local Government, 1970). In this study, the problem of measurement was tackled by starting with a few 'reliable' indicators of social and economic well-being, and then expanding this embryonic operational definition until it covered the required range of urban service functions. Five variables relating to material prosperity and education were selected as 'reliable' indicators of well-being. Subsequently, using data for all settlements of 50 000 or more in England and Wales, corre-lation coefficients were computed between these variables and sixty-eight other variables relating to various social facilities. From the results of this analysis, fifteen variables with high inter-correlations with the 'reliable indicators were selected such that each of seven major urban service functions (administration, education, welfare, cultural recreation, entertainment, physical recreation, and retail distribution) was covered. These fifteen were then added to the five original variables to constitute the final operational definition of level of living:

A. *'Reliable' indicators of well-being*
    (1) annual personal incomes
    (2) households with 2 or more cars
    (3) dwellings of £200 or more rateable value
    (4) product of 1*d*. rate/population
    (5) professional workers

B. *Social facilities which indicate high 'standards' of living*
    (in order of significance)
    (1) doctors' and dentists' surgeries
    (2) golf courses
    (3) quality restaurants
    (4) museums and art galleries
    (5) cinemas
    (6) Marks and Spencer's stores
    (7) clinics, hospitals, nursing homes, etc.
    (8) public libraries
    (9) specialized libraries
    (10) luxury hotels
    (11) stadia and athletic tracks
    (12) universities
    (13) theatres
    (14) restaurants
    (15) county administrative offices

These variables are used to assess variations in levels of living between the nine Economic Planning Regions of England and Wales. Relative access to the fifteen social facilities is illustrated by a series of maps showing the degree of regional self-sufficiency (or deficiency) in relation to a theoretical level of consumer demand based on the socio-economic and age structure of each region. In this way, some allowance is made for the different needs of each region. Although no over-all measure is attempted, it proved possible to reach some broad but interesting conclusions about regional variations in levels of living for the series of distributions:

The South-East scores consistently high on indices of material prosperity and good education but in terms of the range of opportunities for social activity its difference is by no means as vast as popular opinion . . . would make it appear. If the number of potential consumers is considered, the South-East is in fact seriously deficient in some facilities.

The standard [level] of living does not decrease in relation with distance from London or from the main axis of industrial development stretching between London, Birmingham and Merseyside. The peripheral regions of the South-West, Wales, the North and East Anglia may not score highly on indices of material prosperity, but because they have a large number of holiday resorts they appear to have an ample range and quantity of facilities for recreation, entertainment, and other social activity. (Ministry of Housing and Local Government, 1970: 51.)

## Towards a working definition of level of living

These studies of level of living provide a useful background for formulating a working definition of the concept which could be used to investigate spatial variations in well-being within England and Wales at a much finer level of resolution. Before proceeding to such an investigation, however, it is important that the concept is adequately defined. While several studies offer some clarification, the details of definition will clearly vary with the location, date, and scale of investigation. Nevertheless, some features are accepted as integral parts of any definition of level of living. In so far as it relates to the actual satisfaction of the needs and wants of the population, for example, the concept is unambiguous. It is also generally accepted that level of living should be regarded as more than just the equivalent of goods and services relating to those needs and wants, since it is clear that many aspects of leisure and security, for example, cannot be classed as consumers' goods or services. Furthermore, it is widely accepted that the concept derives from, and can be disaggregated into, a number of discrete classes of needs and wants which are aspired to by the population as a whole. In relation to England and Wales, the main classes of such needs and wants can be regarded as education health, housing, employment, and material affluence, together with social status, leisure, security, and social stability (Knox, 1974b).

Where level of living is to be defined in relation to large units of population (i.e. regions or cities, as opposed to families or individuals), there

are additional factors to consider. Certain aspects of demographic structure and physical environment, for example, are directly relevant to the
ability or likelihood of satisfying the main classes of needs and wants
outlined above. The physical environment, for instance, directly affects
certain aspects of both health and leisure, whilst the movement of population between areas alters the relative local demand for, and supply of,
labour, housing, and public services. Bearing these considerations in mind
a working definition of level of living for the British context may be put
forward as follows:

'The level of living of persons resident within a given geographical
area is constituted by the over-all composition of housing, health,
education, social status, employment, affluence, leisure, social security,
and social stability aggregately exhibited in that area, together with
those aspects of demographic structure, general physical environment,
and democratic participation which may determine the extent to which
needs the desires relating to the foregoing constituents of level of
living can be, or are, met.'

This definition forms the basis from which an operational definition
has been drawn up and applied to the major local authority areas of
England and Wales in an attempt to initiate a prototype measure of territorial well-being: an informative territorial social indicator which could
eventually be developed into a more ambitious policy-related system for
monitoring national and regional well-being.

# 4 The geography of level of living in England and Wales

'Many spatial variations . . . are to be observed that would surely be unacceptable severally or separately to an *informed*, democratic society, claiming equality of opportunity as one of its goals.' (Coates and Rawstron, 1971: 289.)

This chapter outlines the results of a preliminary attempt to assess the extent of spatial variation in levels of living in England and Wales in 1961 At the outset it should be stressed that the exercise is largely exploratory in nature, and is by no means intended as a definitive statement of terri- torial well-being. It is restricted on the one hand by problems of measure- ment, and on the other by the lack of suitable data. Nevertheless, it is hoped that the results will go at least some way towards illuminating the disparate and unjust patterns of prosperity, welfare, and opportunity that exist within contemporary Britain; patterns which reflect the limi- tations of past policies and patterns which must be identified in order to pave the way for effective decision-making in central and local governmen

Spatial variations in level of living can only be measured indirectly: by a balanced set of variables which constitute an operational definition of the concept. At this stage it is useful to clarify some of the terminology used. The working definition established at the end of Chapter 3 recog- nizes more than ten *constituents* of level of living, such as housing, health and education. These constituents are themselves comprised of a number of *aspects*; the teaching environment and the extent of further education, for example, are both important aspects of education. Each aspect can often be expressed in terms of a wide range of *indicants*: further educatic for example, could be expressed in terms of university places, the number of pupils staying on at school after the legal minimum age, or the pro- portion of adults holding degrees or diplomas. Finally, each indicant becomes a *variable* only when precisely stated in a form that is measurabl on some interval scale and is related to the 'population at risk' (i.e. the population specifically associated with a particular indicant; for example, it is only that part of the population aged between 16 and 25 that is 'at

† This chapter is based on research undertaken by the author whilst at the University of Sheffield (see Knox 1972 and 1974c).

risk' when current levels of further education are being measured).

Table 4.1 lists the constituents, aspects, and indicants from which the operational definition of level of living is derived. The fifty-three variables constituting the operational definition are detailed by Knox (1974c). In general, the scope of the variables is sufficient to provide a reasonably well balanced representation of the concept, despite the restrictions imposed by the availability of data at the scale of the major local authority areas which provide the analytical framework for the study. However, it is important to bear in mind that the success of all subsequent analysis hinges on the quality of the operational definition. Indicants for which data were not available include the possession of consumer durables such as television sets and washing machines, the provision of household power supplies, cooking facilities, central heating and garage space, and the incidence of mental ill-health. Moreover, the quality of available data is, in many cases, far from perfect. In addition, there are several aspects of level of living which would be difficult to quantify objectively. These include landscape quality, job satisfaction, and the general level of contentment with life. Accepting that it is not possible to quantify some aspects of level of living, it must be admitted that some or all of the non-measurable aspects may be important in determining or describing spatial variations in levels of living. The use of only measurable aspects in formulating an operational definition therefore implies the assumption that the correlation between the measurable and non-measurable aspects is high enough to give useful results derived solely from the former. Finally, it should be noted that indicants of several important constituents of level of living are excluded from the operational definition because they are not subject to significant variations from person to person or from place to place within England and Wales. The most important of these are the basic human freedoms of expression, politics, or religion, together with adequate basic levels of literacy, nutrition, and clothing.

## Regional variations in levels of living in 1961

The magnitude and complexity of the matrix of raw data compiled from the fifty-three variables (primary variables) for the 145 administrative counties and county boroughs in England and Wales clearly require some kind of synthesis before it is possible to appreciate the spatial expression of level of living. The first stage in this process has been achieved by way of correlation analysis. The results of this analysis

TABLE 4.1

The Indicants of Level of Living used for Local Authorities in England and Wales

| Constituent | Aspect | Indicant |
|---|---|---|
| A. Housing | Occupancy characteristics | (1) Occupational density |
| | | (2) Overcrowding |
| | | (3) Shared dwellings |
| | | (4) Vacant dwellings |
| | | (5) Small households |
| | | (6) Large households |
| | | (7) Owner-occupied dwellings |
| | | (8) Privately rented unfurnished dwellings |
| | | (9) Local authority rented dwellings |
| | Quality of housing | (10) Rateable values |
| | | (11) Cold water supplies |
| | | (12) Hot water supplies |
| | | (13) Access to water closet |
| | | (14) Access to fixed bath |
| | Housebuilding | (15) Total new houses |
| | | (16) New local authority houses |
| B. Health | Disease | (17) Infant mortality |
| | | (18) Mortality from bronchitis |
| | | (19) Mortality from tuberculosis |
| | Access to medical care | (20) List-Sizes of Principal General Medical Practitioners |
| | | (21) School dentists |
| C. Education | Extended Education | (22) Adults who left school before the age of 15 |
| | | (23) Pupils staying on at school |
| | Teaching environment | (24) Senior school teachers per pupil |
| | | (25) Junior school teachers |

D. Social Status — Social Status
(26) Professional and managerial workers
(27) Manual workers

E. Employment — Use of Labour
(28) Unemployment
(29) Economically active population
(30) Female activity rate

F. Affluence — Money income
(31) Low personal incomes
(32) High personal incomes
— Consumption
(33) Retail trade
(34) Car ownership

G. Leisure — Access to facilities
(35) Libraries
(36) Cinemas
(37) Restaurants
(38) Hotels

H. Social Security — Safety
(39) Police services
— Welfare
(40) Welfare accommodation
(41) Children's services

I. Social Stability — Crime
(42) Indictable offences
— Family stability
(43) Divorce
(44) Illegitimacy

J. Demographic Structure — Age and life cycle
(45) Age group 0–14
(46) Age group 15–44
(47) Age group 60+
— Population change and mobility
(48) Natural population change
(49) Migration balance
(50) Residence in one area since birth

K. General Physical Environment — Urbanism
(51) Persons per acre

L. Democratic Participation — Democratic Participation
(52) Unopposed seats in local elections
(53) Size of poll in local elections

suggested that there were important similarities in the geographic distribution of some aspects and indicants of level of living (Knox, 1974c). A
number of variables—particularly those relating to average occupational
density (persons per room), access to a fixed bath, manual workers, and
mortality from bronchitis—has substantial average inter-correlations with
the 52 other variables. Since these values were derived from a large number
of moderately high correlations rather than from a few very high correlations, it is reasonable to assume the existence of some general spatial
patterns associated with levels of living. In order to resolve these patterns,
principal components analysis was used. The mechanics and rationale of
technique are described in detail by a number of authors (Harman, 1967;
Rummel, 1967). It is a technique which has already proved popular in
attempts to develop social indicators because it enables a large set of
variables to be efficiently reduced to a small number of new variables
(called components) which are derived directly from the original variables
and which account for a large proportion of the variation in the original
data.

The analysis revealed six important components, the first three of
which are clearly identifiable with certain socio-grographic processes.
These three may be regarded as the most distinctive elements of the
spatial expression of level of living in England and Wales. Predictably, the
first (and most important) component is a general component. It is a
product of several constituents of level of living and in this sense could
be termed a 'level of living' component. Social status, health, housing,
employment, and affluence are all represented strongly, whilst its over-all
spatial expression reflects a marked relationship with urbanism. In general,
urban areas, particularly those which have been urbanized and industrialized for the longest period of time, have the worst levels of living on the
basis of this component. Most county boroughs, in fact, score worse-than-
average, the exceptions consisting of resort towns such as Bournemouth,
Southend-on-Sea, and Blackpool. This association with urbanism affords
an interesting comparison with the results of similar analyses of socio-
geographic data at more detailed scales (such as studies of the factorial
ecology of cities), where the comprehensive influence of social class is
often reflected by a first component or factor which is more specifically
related to social-class variables.

The second component, however, does have parallels in other socio-
geographic studies. It is closely related to variables measuring age struc-

ture, family stability, and household composition: a distinctive complex which is often revealed in studies of urban ecology and commonly designated as reflective of 'familism' or 'life-cycle' (Timms, 1971). The broad expression of the component is such that the worst-off areas (those with a high degree of family instability, a predominantly old age structure, high proportions of single-person households and shared dwellings) cover most of south-eastern and south-western England as well as most of the coastal resort towns and a number of intermediate-sized towns such as Blackburn, Rochdale, Reading, and Oxford.

The third component, although relatively less important, is particularly interesting. It is closely related to a collection of variables which together suggest an association with suburbanization (high rates of house construction, overcrowding in junior schools, low levels of unemployment, underprovision of cinemas, few dwellings lacking basic household amenities). This is supported by the spatial expression of the component: the highest-scoring areas are the administrative counties encompassing the urbanized and industrialized centres of southern, south-eastern, central, and north-western England. They are areas which have attracted large numbers of people because of their relative economic prosperity; conversely, people have been less willing or unable to establish new residences within the larger urban centres. It should, however, be stressed that this component may owe its existence to the boundaries of the local authority areas as much as anything else, since the boundaries of most county boroughs in England and Wales in 1961 were less than generous, leaving their more prosperous outer areas within the jurisdiction of the adjacent administrative counties.

*An index*

Individual components, despite their importance, are unwieldy measures of what is essentially a unitary concept. It is therefore desirable, if possible, to construct some over-all measure of level of living. The 'component scores' produced by the components analysis (see Rummel, 1967) offer a potentially useful basis for an over-all measure: a simple index could be derived from the summation of the six component scores for each local authority. This depends, however, upon the components being unambiguous in character, which is not possible in this case because several of the primary variables are not entirely normative. Besides, using only normative variables can easily produce components with an ambiguous character. Without using the actual component scores, however, it is still possible to make use of the valuable information provided by the components analysis by constructing an over-all measure from a small number of 'diagnostic' variables. These variables are selected so as to represent, between them, the character and composition of the major components. In this case the diagnostic variables have been selected such that each is highly associated with at least one of the six components (with a correlation of ± 0·600 or more) and has a large proportion (at least 75 per cent) of its variance involved in the over-all component structure. Within this framework, the number of diagnostic variables used is necessarily arbitrary, and their selection subjective. An index derived from only four diagnostic variables was found to be as effective as indices derived from other combinations of various numbers of alternatives (Knox, 1972). The four are:

1. the average number of persons per room
2. the percentage of households without exclusive use of a fixed bath
3. the percentage of economically active persons out of employment
4. the percentage of persons aged 60 or more.

Index values for each local authority have been computed from rank-scores on each of these variables, such that low index values are indicative of a high level of living. The resultant range of values extend from 9·7 in Buckinghamshire (the best) to 83·9 in Gateshead (the worst). In general, the spatial distribution of index values does not contradict or challenge accepted ideas about the socio-economic geography of England and Wales: low levels of living are found in Wales, south-western and north-eastern England, Lancashire, and East Anglia; and high levels of living are found in the counties of central and southern England and the Midlands (Fig. 4.1). One important qualification to this generalization, however, is that the county of London, which for a long time has been popularly regarded as relatively well off, has a very high index value (70·1). With a population of 3·2 millions involved, the implications of this are really very serious. Clearly the over-all level of living in metro-politan London does not match the availability of theatres, hotels, restaurants, department stores, museums, art galleries, libraries, adminis-trative headquarters, and specialist services in central London upon which the idea of a prosperous and healthy London must largely be based.

On a regional basis, it is possible to distinguish an area of high levels of living extending from the Home Counties towards Somerset, Cheshire,

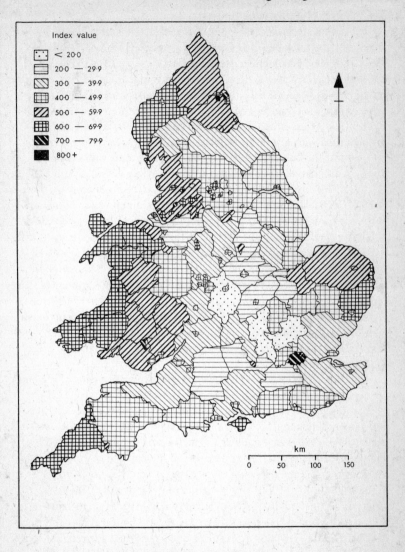

FIG. 4.1  An index of level of living for England and Wales.
*Source*: After Knox (1974c).

and Nottinghamshire. Within this area, the majority of county boroughs tend towards intermediate levels of living, although Oxford, Croydon, West Bromwich, Dudley, and Worcester are equally well off, whilst Stoke-on-Trent, Nottingham, Reading, East Ham, and West Ham stand out with relatively poor scores. The best areas are administrative counties which possess large tracts of rich agricultural land as well as containing many prosperous suburbs and satellites of larger industrial and commercial centres. At the other extreme, two different sorts of area can be distinguished with low levels of living. Most numerous are the county boroughs of the industrial north, amongst which some of the worst scores of all are recorded—Gateshead (83·9), Wigan (78·9), South Shields (74·2), St. Helens (69·7), Newcastle upon Tyne (69·4), Rochdale (69·3), Halifax (68·9)—and where the legacy of inter-war depression combined with the continued decline in the coal-mining, shipbuilding, and textile industries is reflected by the over-all level of living. A second type of area is made up of administrative counties in western Wales, plus Cornwall and Cumberland. Many reasons may be put forward in explanation of the low levels of living in these areas. Amongst them are remoteness, economic dependence on marginal agriculture, the burden of dependency created by the in-migration of retired persons to coastal areas combined with the out-migration of younger persons seeking a wider range of opportunities, and the problems of seasonal employment associated with the tourist industry.

In relation to post-war policies aimed at tackling problems of regional imbalance, Fig. 4.1 is most illuminating. Between 1945 and the early 1960s a number of policy instruments were employed by the central government, including factory building, improvements to public services, loans to industrial estate companies and specific industrial undertakings, and the use of Industrial Development Certificates. These were specially designed to assist the depressed areas designated as Development Areas in the Distribution of Industry Acts of 1945, 1950, and 1958. In the same period, the building of New-Towns was seen as an important contribution towards alleviating problems of congestion in the major conurbations. The Development Areas in England and Wales consisted of south Wales, Wrexham, Merseyside, Wigan, St. Helens, north-east Lancashire, Cumberland, and a large tract of the North-East, including Tyneside, Wearside, and Teeside. Fig. 4.1 shows that in 1961 these were still among the worst-off areas in terms of level of living. Moreover, many areas had equally low levels of living although they themselves were not assisted areas. In particular, London, Humberside, south Yorkshire, the Potteries, much of the West Yorkshire conurbation, Lancashire, rural Wales, Cornwall, and East Anglia appeared to be as depressed, in an over-all sense, as the Development Areas. Significantly, some of these areas have since been scheduled for regional aid, whilst the expansion of the New Town/over-spill programme around London, together with large-scale urban renewal programmes, has undoubtedly alleviated some of the problems of inner London. Nevertheless, there still remain a number of areas which were depressed in 1961 and which have received no outside help in catching up with the rest of the country. Without some policy-related system of measuring well-being, these places—the likes of Barnsley, Bradford, Kingston upon Hull, and Stoke-on-Trent—are likely to fall irretrievably behind in the scramble for better living standards, unnoticed by all except those who, through no fault of their own, happen to live in them.

## A classification

Another useful approach to the spatial expression of levels of living is to classify the local authorities according to their scores on the diagnostic variables, thus producing a 'typology' based on the major dimensions of spatial variations in levels of living. This has been effected by the statistical techniques of cluster analysis and multiple discriminant analysis. Details of these techniques may be found in most texts dealing with multivariate techniques—see, for example, Cooley and Lohnes (1964), Kendall (1957), and Sokal and Sneath (1963). Twelve distinctive types of local authorities are shown in Table 4.2, whilst the differences between the groups are illustrated by Fig. 4.2, which shows the average standardized scores (Z-scores) for each group on each of the four diagnostic variables. These twelve groups cannot be ordered from 'good' to 'bad' along any finite continuum (although the 'best' is clearly group 1 and the 'worst' groups 10–12), but they add considerably to our ability to comprehend spatial variations in levels of living. For example, although the area of higher levels of living identified on Fig. 4.1 corresponds broadly with the distribution of local authorities in 'better' groups (1–6), the converse does not hold: ten of the constituents of group 2 have values between 30·0 and 39·9, and twelve have values between 40·0 and 49·9. Moreover, as index values converge towards the average, more groups are involved: groups, 2, 3, 4, 5, and 6 are all represented in the range 40·0

TABLE 4.2

*A Classification of Local Authorities Based on Four Diagnostic Variables*

Group  1 :

Berkshire
Buckinghamshire
Hertfordshire
Huntingdonshire
Leicestershire

Nottinghamshire
Oxfordshire
Oxford
Rutland
Warwickshire

Group  2 :

Bedfordshire
Cambridgeshire
Carlisle
Chester
Cheshire
Croydon
Derbyshire
Essex
Gloucester
Gloucestershire
Hampshire
Ipswich
Kesteven

Leeds
Lincoln
Lindsey
Middlesex
Northamptonshire
Shropshire
Surrey
Wakefield
West Riding
Wiltshire
Worcestershire
Worcester
York

Group  3 :

Bath
Bristol
Canterbury
Derby
Dorset
East Riding
East Suffolk
Kent

Leicester
Norfolk
Northampton
Norwich
Portsmouth
Reading
Somerset
West Suffolk

Group  4 :

Barrow
Breconshire
Bury
Cardiff
Cumberland
Darlington
Denbighshire
Doncaster
Exeter

Flintshire
Grimsby
Lancashire
North Riding
Peterborough
Southampton
Southend-on-Sea
Swansea
Wallasey

Group  5 :

Birmingham
Coventry
Dudley
Newport
Northumberland
Plymouth

Rotherham
Staffordshire
Walsall
West Bromwich
Wolverhampton

Group  6 :

Bournemouth
Brighton
Devon
Eastbourne

East Sussex
Southport
Westmorland
West Sussex

Table 4.2. Cont.

| Group  7 : | Blackburn | Holland |
|---|---|---|
| | Bolton | Huddersfield |
| | Bradford | Isle of Ely |
| | Burnley | Nottingham |
| | Burton-on-Trent | Preston |
| | Dewsbury | Sheffield |
| | East Ham | Smethwick |
| | Halifax | Stockport |
| | Herefordshire | Rochdale |
| Group  8 : | Barnsley | Salford |
| | Birkenhead | Stoke-on-Trent |
| | Glamorganshire | Warrington |
| | Kingston upon Hull | West Hartlepool |
| | Manchester | Wigan |
| | Monmouth | |
| Group  9 : | Blackpool | Great Yarmouth |
| | Caernarvon | Hastings |
| | Carmarthen | Isle of Wight |
| | Cornwall | Pembroke |
| Group 10 : | Durham | St. Helens |
| | Gateshead | South Shields |
| | Liverpool | Sunderland |
| | London | Tynemouth |
| | Newcastle upon Tyne | |
| Group 11 : | Bootle | Oldham |
| | Middlesborough | West Ham |
| Group 12 : | Anglesey | Merthyr Tydfil |
| | Cardiganshire | Montgomeryshire |
| | Merionethshire | Radnorshire· |

*Source*: After Knox (1947c).

to 49·9. These features emphasize the utility of the typology as a comp-lementary measure to the index, especially in relation to near-average index values, where significant variations in the contribution of individual diagnostic variables may be masked by the generality of the index.

Spatially, the typology is also informative. Local authorities in the 'best' groups are located centrally within a large area of generally 'good' groups in central and southern England, but include only parts of south-eastern England, the area traditionally accepted as the most favour-able, socially and economically, within Britain. Several other features are of interest, especially the distinctive resort and retirement areas of groups 6 and 9 and some of the unexpected juxtapositions revealed by the

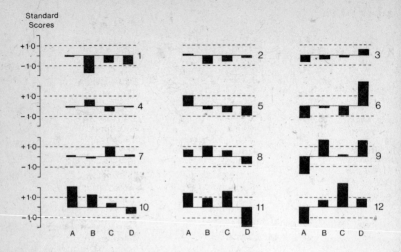

FIG. 4.2   Average characteristics of the twelve groups of local authority areas.
A = Persons per room; B = Unemployment; C = Lack of fixed bath;
D = Persons aged 60+.
Table 4.2 lists the authorities in each group.
*Source*: After Knox (1974c).

grouping procedures. In group 2, with favourable scores on all four
diagnostic variables are Carlisle and Wakefield, pleasant enough places, but
not especially noted for their relative well-being in a national context.
Furthermore, metropolitan London has the same level of living characteristics as Gateshead, Tynemouth, South Shields, Sunderland, and St. Helens
(group 10): whilst the grouping of Herefordshire, Part of Lincolnshire
(Holland) and the Isle of Ely with industrial county boroughs such as
Blackburn, Dewsbury, Halifax, Preston, and Stockport which dominate
group 7 is equally surprising and no more easily explained. It is not within
the scope of this chapter to investigate the reasons for these variations:
rather it is intended simply to illustrate the extent and pattern of spatial
variations in levels of living. In this context, perhaps the most important
feature of the typology is that 70 per cent of the poorer groups (7 to 12)
are county boroughs. That three-quarters of these are located to the north
of a line from the Mersey to the Humber is a forceful affirmation of the
intensity of spatial imbalance in levels of living within England and
Wales.

*Local variations in levels of living*

Having established the existence of broad regional disparities, it is interesting and informative to examine briefly the extent of variations in levels of living at a more detailed scale. For this purpose, data on the four diagnostic variables were collected for the 2946 rural districts, urban districts, municipal boroughs, and wards that formed (in 1961) a nested hierarchy within the major local authority areas. Here we must recognize the implicit assumption that the four variables are equally diagnostic of levels of living at the increased level of resolution. A full account of the investigation is given by Knox (1972). The detail afforded by the change in scale produced some illuminating findings. In particular, although the diagnostic variables were found to have broadly similar spatial distributions at both scales, it was shown that none had values at the county/county borough scale which were entirely accurate in portraying the conditions experienced by a majority of people living within their boundaries. This was particularly marked in larger urban areas, where the internal range of conditions was often almost as great as that for the nation as a whole. In other words, the aggregative nature of the county/county borough data often masked important internal spatial variations. In addition, the detailed information derived from the analysis was useful in pinpointing relationships which were not previously apparent. The influence of public housing on the social geography of England and Wales, for instance, was strongly emphasized. Large council estates were consistently found to generate extreme scores on three of the four diagnostic variables: average occupational densities (high scores), lack of a fixed bath (low scores), and the proportion of older persons (low scores).

The degree of variability within major local authority areas is illustrated by Figs. 4.3 and 4.4 which show the index values for south Wales and the West Yorkshire conurbation respectively. These may be regarded as parts of the same map: the index values and categories of shading have been determined in relation to the complete data set, but obvious difficulties of cartographic representation preclude the presentation of maps for the whole of England and Wales. Without going into the detailed social geography of the two areas, it is apparent that there are enormous variations in living conditions over very small distances. Within south Wales, the intermediate levels of living of the administrative counties of Glamorgan and Monmouth (see Fig. 4.1) are clearly influenced by the zone of low levels of living associated with the coalfield areas and extended from Glyncorrwg and Maesteg in the west to Abertillery and Blaenavon in the east. This area forms a distinctive subdivision of both counties, contrasting sharply with the more prosperous coastal belt. Diversity within the three largest county boroughs is even more marked. Swansea, with an index value of 59·5, can be divided into an eastern half of wards with values greater than 60·0 and a western half with values of less than 50·0; within Cardiff and Newport, although there is no such straightforward spatial pattern, there are even greater disparities, with six of the eight classes of shading represented. The extent of these local variations in impressive although not pleasing.

Within the West Yorkshire conurbation, it is possible to identify the distinctive trends of the geography of well-being in terms of a simple classification of index values above and below 50·0. There is a crescent-shaped area of higher levels of living in the north of the conurbation, extending from northern Halifax through the northern wards of Bradford to Pudsey and the eastern, northern, and western suburbs of Leeds. Outliers of this crescent-shaped area are found in parts of Huddersfield, Dewsbury, and Wakefield, whilst the rest of the conurbation suffers low levels of living. This pattern again makes for a diversity which is not suggested by the index values for the major local authorities (Fig. 4.1). Leeds, for instance, with an intermediate index value of 40·0, contains few sub-areas with such values, being divided into an outer band of wards with low values and a central core of wards with much higher values.

Whilst not detracting from the validity of the results obtained for the major local authority areas, these instances of diversity constitute an important qualification to them, underlining the importance of scale in social geography. At the same time they provide clear illustrations of the extent of spatial disparities in local well-being which must not be ignored if we are to pay more than lip-service to the idea of a just society. In this chapter it has been only possible to give a brief outline of the findings of the study of levels of living in England and Wales, but it should be sufficient to indicate the extent of both regional and local variations in levels of living, and to illustrate the potential of the concept as a framework for the regular monitoring of territorial well-being. Without the information provided by such monitoring, 'ignorance is bliss [and] spatial variations that are unjust, harmful and inefficient are accepted not only by those

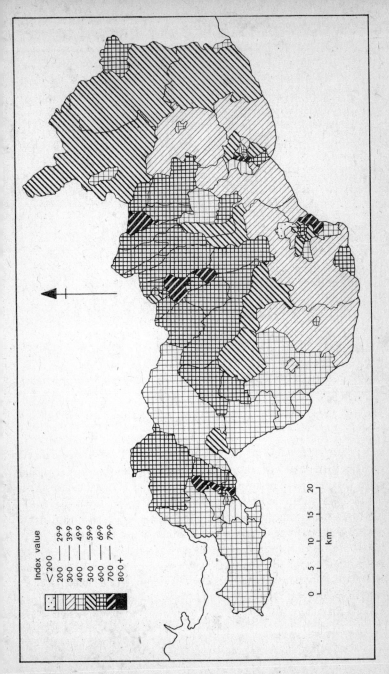

Index value

< 20·0
20·0 — 29·9
30·0 — 39·9
40·0 — 49·9
50·0 — 59·9
60·0 — 69·9
70·0 — 79·9
80·0 +

0    5    10   15   20
          km

FIG. 4.3  Levels of living in South Wales, 1961.

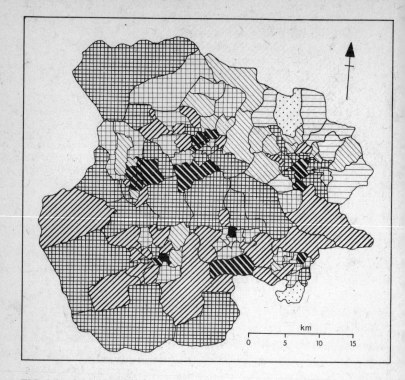

FIG. 4.4   Levels of living in the West Yorkshire conurbation, 1961.
         *Key*: as for Fig. 4.3.

who govern both nationally and locally, but also by those who, did they but know it, suffer badly because they happen to live and work in particular areas' (Coates and Rawstron, 1971). The analysis outlined here is already out of date, but it is unlikely that the *extent* of spatial disparities will have been significantly reduced since the early 1960s, although their pattern may have altered somewhat. It would be relatively simple to repeat the exercise when more recent data become available, but what is really needed is the setting up of a *regular* system of measurement. Until such time, important policy decisions will continue to be made on the basis of insufficient information, and the consequences will be overlooked because there is no official yardstick with which to monitor their success.

# 5    Some conclusions

'As long as the defects of existing data are recognized and improvements are constantly sought a useful start can be made on describing some important dimensions of human existence conspicuously missing from the geographer's conventional view of the world'. (Smith, 1973a: 136.)

This study has attempted to draw attention to the importance of being able to assess well-being in contemporary Western countries such as Britain, where traditional measures of well-being such as consumption per head are increasingly rendered inadequate by changing aspirations and collective preferences. If we do not have more sensitive measures of territorial well-being, we shall not know how successful or efficient territorial policies have been; if we do not initiate the regular measurement of well-being, there will be harmful delays before we know how effective these policies have been. This is of special importance at a time when most of the Western world is experiencing the unusual combination of inflation and recession. If past experience of both is anything to go by, the poor will get relatively worse off and spatial disparities will widen.

Against this background, the aims and potential of social indicators have been outlined and the progress made in developing territorial social indicators, particularly those aimed at an integrated approach to well-being, has been illustrated. It is clear that there is not yet a general consensus of opinion about the conceptualization of well-being or the approach to its measurement. Indeed, there are as many operational definitions of well-being and its various facets as there have been attempts to measure them. To a large extent these variations can be put down to differences in scale and location between the studies involved, whilst methodological difficulties and the shortage of data on many important social conditions account for most of the discrepancies between conceptual adstractions of well-being and the variables representing them. Nevertheless, the lack of a generally accepted conceptual framework around which to build indicators of well-being remains a persistent stumbling-block at both the local and the national level. Level of living has been put forward in this book as the sort of concept which could fulfil this role, and an attempt has been made to define the concept and portray its spatial expression within England and Wales. The fundamental point, however, is not whether the definition put forward here is the best that can be devised, or whether the approach taken to its measurement is the most effective. What is important is that there should be *some* commonly accepted conceptual basis from which operational social indicators can be developed. Subsidiary to this is the suggestion that level of living can provide a useful foundation in this context. Without a basis of this sort, social indicators (and territorial social indicators) will never be more than general-purpose variables, individually useful but collectively ineffective as compatible and comprehensive measures of well-being.

Although we may be a long way from reaching the consensus necessary for establishing a policy-related system of measurement, operational representations of concepts such as the quality of life, social well-being, and level of living form useful descriptive devices. In a spatial framework they are able to portray an important dimension of the social system, revealing the extent to which groups of people in different geographical areas experience different conditions and levels of opportunity in relation to all of the factors impinging on their well-being. Using descriptive devices such as these, it is quite realistic to aim at improved social reporting as a relatively short-term prospect. It was in this spirit that the research by the author was undertaken. The results show that there were considerable variations in well-being within England and Wales in the early 1960s at two significant levels of resolution. Applying the concepts of social well-being and the quality of life, Smith (1973a) and Wilson (1969) respectively have shown that there were also extreme inequalities at a number of spatial levels within the United States in the 1960s. These descriptive approaches to well-being are themselves an improvement to socio-spatial reporting, and it is not too idealistic to envisage such measures as the basis of analyses of social change and even for the prediction of future social conditions. Certainly, Western societies such as Britain and the United States have the resources to achieve this level of sophistication in socio-geographic management. What is not yet certain is whether they will place a high enough priority on eliminating spatial disparities for the agencies of government to become sufficiently committed to this sort of work.

### Filling the gaps

Only with an increased interest on the part of central governments in socio-spatial reporting and management will it be possible to stimulate data-collecting agencies to improve the range and quality of available data. At present, many of the variables used in the construction of social indicators are not direct measures of well-being, but surrogates: for example, good access to health facilities is often used as an indicant of health, but good access does not necessarily make for a healthy population. Of more direct relevance would be measures of the intensity and duration of illnesses experienced by the population, (Culyer, Lavers, and Williams, 1972). Collection of this sort of information, at least in the foreseeable future, will be possible only on a sample-survey basis. In Britain, signs are already appearing that the governmental statistical service is attaching increasing importance to the rule of such surveys, although few have been extensive enough to provide much information for geographical sub-divisions of the country.

Ideally, data relating to well-being should be collected in the form of *flow* data—i.e. as measures of satisfaction per unit of time. Most attempts to develop social indicators and quantitative expressions of well-being have been exploratory, and have used static, cross-sectional analyses as a logical starting-point. But social and economic conditions are subject to continual change, and from an academic standpoint, as well as in relation to decision-making and policy planning, a more relevant approach would be to analyse the rate and direction of changes using flow data. Unfortunately, the reality is that reliable flow data exist for very few aspects of well-being; and for spatial disaggregations of national units they are almost non-existent.

The sort of data we need in order to construct more sophisticated measures of well-being should also ideally relate specifically to *outputs* of the social system rather than inputs. For example, they should relate to improvements in health rather than expenditure on health services, and to improvements in educational levels rather than to attendance at school. In short, they should relate to ends rather than means. Moser (1971) sees the difficulties involved in developing output measures as one of the main challenges facing the social-indicators movement. One of the major conceptual difficulties is that there are often ends which can also be regarded as means. In this sense school attendance is an intermediate end; but it is really a means to the end of improved education.

Indicators of well-being should also ideally take account of the *distribution* of satisfaction among the population. Here we must involve ourselves in value judgements, for we must decide what sort of distribution is optimal in terms of the well-being of community; we can choose, for example, between an even distribution, one that is based on need (however defined), or one that is based on achievement. In Western societies egalitarian distribitions are generally seen as the most desirable. In this context, any unit of resources transferred from the satisfaction of wants of the affluent to the needs of the non-affluent may be seen as increasing over-all well-being. Put this way, the political implications are more explicit. Once the problem is resolved, a distribution coefficient of some sort can be built into the indicators. The calculation of the coefficient would clearly depend on the criterion of distributive justice to be applied. Probably the most satisfactory coefficient for an egalitarian criterion would be one derived from the familiar Lorenz concerntration curve (Smith, 1973b).

Above all, though, we lack adequate means of measuring satisfactions against commonly accepted and objectively established parameters of need. Culyer, Lavers, and Williams (1972) have shown that it is possible to construct indicators geared to needs, but the difficulties involved in determining need in relation to the whole range of components of well-being mean that the whole question is likely to remain unresolved until the systematic measurement of well-being has gathered real momentum.

## Social reporting and social planning

Indicators with even some of these qualities would go a long way towards enabling the establishment of a regular and detailed policy-related system of measurement. The potential role of such a system within a simplified framework of national and regional planning is shown by Fig. 5.1. At the national level, an over-all measure of well-being, such as an index of living, would constitute part of a comprehensive information system aimed at furnishing anough data for an enlightened assessment of national priorities in relation to national goals, national resources, aggregate demand, and collective preferences. At the regional level, measures of well-being would enable a close monitoring of the changing socio-economic geography of the country and thus provide the basis for a well-informed approach to the formulation of territorial policies and a yardstick for assessing the effectiveness of past policies.

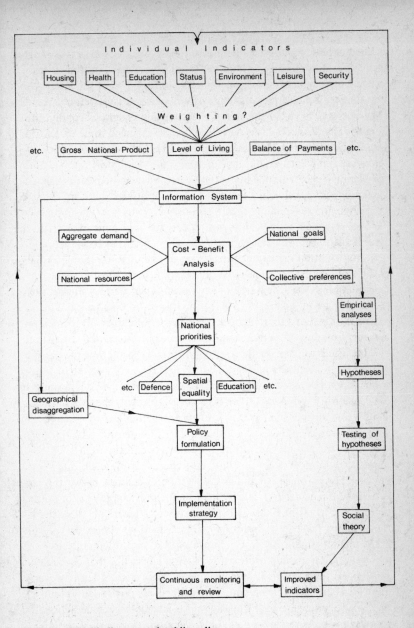

FIG. 5.1  Social indicators and public policy.
        *Source*: After Knox (1974b).

Several points require clarification. Firstly, such a system falls short of the social accounting systems envisaged by the more optimistic proponents of social indicators, since no account is taken of the interrelationships between the various elements of well-being; it is therefore a social reporting system rather than a social accounting system. Secondly, the implications of the 'cost—benefit' box in Fig. 5.1 need some elucidation. Basically, it need represent no more than a well-informed allocation of resources and priorities, but it also reflects the managerial rationale of the planning-programming-budgeting systems which are increasingly becoming part of all policy decisions. Quite obviously there are dangers in applying these techniques too rigorously in fields involving human welfare, and there have been strong objections from some quarters to the 'new Philistinism' that can reduce all human conditions to pounds and pence on a nation's shopping list. Although attempts to rationalize the process of making decisions must be welcome, there must be self-examination in the acceptance of such techniques. Besides all else, such techniques are by no means easy for the layman to understand. This makes the ideal of a participatory democracy more difficult to achieve, and therefore places more power in the hands of the technocratic élite.

This brings us back to the question of priorities and how they are arrived at. It is an issue of major controversy since although there is a wide measure of agreement about those categories of needs and wants that constitute well-being, there is no such agreement about priorities. Thus 'value judgements have to be made as whether a cancer-free society with illiteracy is better or worse than a fully literate society with cancer. Of course, the choices are seldom framed as specifically as this. But financial resources are continually being allocated and re-allocated— between law enforcement and anti-poverty programmes, between weapon systems and medical care—according to some prevailing social or political philosophy.' (Smith, 1973a: 138.) One way of interpreting priorities is via consumer behaviour; in this way the satisfactions chosen by consumers in the market-place are seen as a direct expression of their collective preferences. An implicit assumption of this approach is that consumers are the best judges of their own well-being. In most societies, however, there are some satisfactions which are collectively demanded but not available for exchange in the market-place. Examples include national parks and welfare services of all kinds. The priorities assigned to these satisfactions clearly cannot be gauged from consumer behaviour. The usual solution is for a person or group of persons 'who know best' (politicians, civil servants, etc.) to judge the priorities, an approach which is seen by some to contain an undesirable élitist or paternalistic element. The alternative would be for priorities to be determined by some regular survey of attitudes and preferences.

Finally, in relation to the whole question of measuring well-being we must recognize that there may be a considerable difference between an individual's own judgement of his or her degree of satisfaction or well-being and that of an outsider's (based on conventional 'hard' data). Many consider perceived well-being to be the best criterion of whether society is well or not, since it may be the only way of avoiding the biased values of academics, planners, and politicians concerned with interpreting indicators based on 'hard' data (Abrams, 1972). An equally tenable, and perhaps more satisfactory, approach would be to weight the 'hard' data according to the relative significance of various aspects of well-being as seen by the society in question. This is clearly another reason for the investigation of collective preferences. Once established, these preferences could form a common link between the weighting system for social indicators and the priorities given to public policies.

## Geography and territorial well-being

The output of a regular system of measurement of territorial well-being would be useful not only for socio-geographic management but also for teaching and research in geography. It would be especially relevant to the 'problem-solving' and 'socially relevant' approach to geography that has emerged in the 1970s. That such an approach is desirable is not universally accepted. There are some quantitative geographers who find in it an unacceptable degree of subjectivity, whilst to others it threatens the tradition of academic objectivity and detachment (Trewartha, 1973). But the techniques of the 'new' geography, having established their utility in the 1960s, now need to be directed towards substantial, real-world problems if they are to fulfil their real potential. As to the question of academic detachment, the acceptance of spatial variations in well-being as the focal point of geographic inquiry 'requires no dedication to the promotion of social change, or to leftist politics. It simply requires recognition of what is surely the self-evident truth that, if human beings are the object of our curiosity in human geography, then the quality of their lives is of paramount interest'. (Smith, 1973b: 112.)

If this is the case, the first task of a socially responsible human geography is the accurate portrayal of spatial variations in well-being. But as soon as attention is concentrated on these variations, ethical questions arise which cannot easily be avoided. Mapping inequable distributions is bound to raise the question of whether or not they are just. Harvey (1972a) has examined the idea of territorial distributive justice in detail, pointing out that the justness of a given distribution depends, in the first instance, on the criterion of distributive justice to be applied: equality, need, achievement, etc. Assuming that it is possible to decide upon an appropriate or desirable criterion, the geographer faced with an unjust distribution must decide whether he is under an obligation to help society improve the situation. Traditionally, it has been sufficient to describe and explain the situation, without becoming further involved. Recently, however, Harvey (1972b, 1973) has vigorously and persuasively led a growing lobby for greater commitment amongst geographers to spatial social justice, a commitment which is explicitly directed towards revolutionizing societies which tolerate and perpetuate these injustices, and a commitment which also demands a 'revolution' in geographic thought. Whatever the preferred balance between 'relevance' and 'revolution', territorial social indicators of the sort described and illustrated in this study can play an important role in awakening more people to the extent of spatial disparities in well-being and, it is hoped, promote a more active involvement in social reforms.

# References and further reading

Abrams, M. (1972). 'Social indicators and social equity', *New Society*, 22, 454–5.

Central Advisory Council for Education (England) (1967). *Children and their Primary Schools* (Plowden Report), H.M.S.O., London.

Carlisle, E. (1972). 'The conceptual structure of social indicators', in Shonfield and Shaw pp. 23–32.

Coates, B. E., and Rawstron, E. M. (1971). *Regional Variations in Britain*, Batsford, London.

Cooley, W. W. and Lohnes, P. R. (1964). *Multivariate Procedures for the Behavioural Sciences*, Wiley, New York.

Cullingworth, J. B. (1972). *Problems of an Urban Society*, Volume II: *The Social Content of Planning*, Allen and Unwin London.

Culyer, A. J., Lavers, R. J., and Williams, A. (1972). 'Health Indicators', in Shonfield and Shaw (1972), 94—118.
Drewnowski, J. (1970). *Measuring the Level of Living*, paper delivered to the Town and Country Planning Summer School, Swansea.
— and Scott, W. (1968). 'The level of living index', *Ekistics*, **25**, 266—75.
Duncan, O. D., Cuzzort, R. P., and Duncan, B. (1961) *Statistical Geography: problems in analysing areal data*, Free Press, New York.
Edwards, J. (1973). 'Social indicators and social policy', *Schedule*, **2**, 18—23.
Flax, M. J. (1972). *A Study in Comparative Urban Indicators*: *conditions in 18 large Metropolitan Areas*, The Urban Institute, Washington, D.C.
Gordon, I. R., and Whittaker, R. M. (1972). 'Indicators of local prosperity in the South-West region', *Regional Studies*, **6**, 299—313.
Greater London Council (1969). *Greater London Development Plan*,
Hagood, M. J., and Bowles, G. K. (1957). 'Farm Operator level of living indexes for the United States', in *Major Statistical Series of the U.S.D.A. —How they are constructed and used*, Part 7, Farm Population Employment and Levels of Living, United States Department of Agriculture, Agricultural Handbook No. 118, Washington, D.C.
Harman, H. (1967). *Modern Factor Analysis*, University of Chicago Press,
Harvey, D. (1972a). 'Social justice and spatial systems', in Peet, R. (ed), *Geographical Perspectives on American Poverty*, Antipode Monographs in Social Geography, 1, Worcester, Mass., 87—106.
— (1972b). 'Revolutionary and Counter-Revolutionary Theory in Geography and the problem of ghetto formation', *Antipode*, **4**, 1—18
— (1973). *Social Justice and the City*, Arnold, London.
Kamrany, N. M., and Christakis, A. N. (1970). 'Social indicators in perspective' *Socio-Economic Planning Sciences*, **14**, 207—16.
Kendall, M. G. (1957). *A Course in Multivariate Analysis*, Griffith, London.
King, L. J. (1969). *Statistical Analysis in Geography*, Prentice-Hall, Englewood Cliffs, N.J.
Knox, P. L. (1972). 'Spatial Variations in Level of Living in England and Wales in 1961', unpublished Ph.D. thesis, University of Sheffield, Department of Geography.
— (1974a). 'Social indicators and the concept of level of living' *Sociological Review*, **22**, 249—57.
— (1974b). Level of Living: a conceptual framework for monitoring regional variations in well-being', *Regional Studies*, **8**, 11—19.
— (1974c). 'Spatial variations in level of living in England and Wales in 1961', *Transactions, Institute of British Geographers*, **62**, 1—24.
Land, K. S. (1970). 'Social Indicators', in Smith, R. B. (ed.), *Social Science Methods*, Free Press, New York.
Lewis, G. M. (1968). 'Levels of living in the north-eastern United States *c.* 1960: A new approach to regional geography', *Transactions, Institute of British Geographers*, **45**, 11—37.

Little, A., and Mabey, C. (1972). 'An index for designation of Educational Priority Areas', in Shonfield and Shaw (1972), 67–93.

Lomas, G. (1973). 'London's housing needs, current problems and prospects', in London Council of Social Service, *London's Housing Needs: today's situation and current problems and prospects*, London Council of Social Service, London.

Ministry of Housing and Local Government (1970). *Regional Comparisons in the Standard of Living in England and Wales*, Urban Planning Directorate 3, London.

Moser, C. A. (1970). 'Measuring the quality of life', *New Society*, 428, 1042–3.

— (1971). *Social Indicators: systems, methods and problems,* paper delivered to the International Association for Research in Income and Wealth, Stockholm.

—and Scott, W. (1961). *British Towns—a statistical study of their social and economic differences*, Oliver and Boyd, London.

Perle, E. D. (1970). 'Local societal indicators: a progress report', *Proceedings of the Social Statistics Section*, American Statistical Association, 114–20.

Pipping, H. E. (1953). 'Standards of Living. The concept and its place in economics', in *Commentationes humanarum Litterarum*, 18, No. 4, Helsinki.

The President's Commission on National Goals (1960). *Goals for Americans Report of the President's Commission on National Goals,* Prentice-Hall, Englewood Cliffs, N.J.

Rivlin, A. M. (1971). *Systematic Thinking for Social Action,* The Brookings Institution, Washington, D.C.

Royal Commission on Local Government in England (1969). *Report of the Royal Commission on Local Government in England 1966–1969*, Cmnd. 4040, Volume I: H.M.S.O., London.

Rummel, R. J. (1967). 'Understanding Factor Analysis', *Journal of Conflict Resolution*, 11, 444–80.

Runciman, W. G. (1966). *Relative Deprivation and Social Justice*, Routledge and Kegan Paul, London.

Rural Sociological Society Ad Hoc Committee on Rural Levels and Standards of Living (1956). 'Sociological research in rural levels and standards of living', *Rural Sociology*, 21, 183–95.

Shonfield, A., and Shaw, S. (1972). *Social Indicators and Social Policy*, Heinemann, London.

Smith, D. M. (1973a). *The Geography of Social Well-Being in the United States*, McGraw-Hill, New York.

— (1973b). *An Introduction to Welfare Geography,* Department of Geography and Environmental Studies, University of Witwatersrand, Occasional Paper No. 11.

Sokal, R. R., and Sneath, P. H. A. (1963). *Principles of Numerical Taxonomy*, Freeman, San Francisco.

Terleckyj, N. E. (1970). 'Measuring progress towards social goals: some possibilities at national and local levels', *Management Science*, **16**, B, 765–78.

Timms, D. (1971). *The Urban Mosaic*, Cambridge University Press,

Trewartha, G. (1973). 'Comments on Gilbert White's article "Geography and Public Policy" ', *Professional Geographer*, **25**, 78–9.

United States Department of Health, Education and Welfare (1969). *Towards a Social Report,* U.S. Government Printing Office, Washington, D.C.

Wilson, J. O. (1969). *Quality of Life in the United States: an excursion into the new frontier of socio-economic indicators*, Midwest Research Institute, Kansas City, Mo.

# Index